THE PLANETARY MEDITATIONS

THREE CD AND BOOK SET
BY MICHELLE MANY

Holistic Mountain

COPYRIGHT PAGE

Reviews For The Planetary Meditations

"Michelle Many's voice is beautiful, melodic, soothing and inspiring. "The Planetary Meditations" are a wonderful way to find connection to the planets. Her loving voice along with the soothing music bring our minds into alignment with the music of the spheres. This is a gorgeous work and one which will provide inspiration and healing to all who partake of it. Well done and simply delicious, Michelle! I love it!"

Lynda Hill – author of "360 Degrees of Wisdom": "Charting Your Destiny With the Sabian Oracle" published by Penguin NY.

"Michelle Many's "Planetary Meditations" offer a journey through the solar system and the planetary influences that will indeed shift consciousness. The images possess a vividness that captures one's mind and leads one on a journey that changes perceptions in a delightfully subtle manner. Consider it the Music of the Spheres for the mind."

Philip Sedgwick – noted astrologer and author of "The Sun at the Center" and also his newest work, "Glimpses".

CONTENTS

CONTENTS, continued

What the Planetary Book is and How it is Used

The Planetary Book is to be used along with the Planetary Meditation CD Set. The book is designed to be used as a tool for healing and growth. The questions are specifically created to promote change and bring focus to your life.

Turn up the volume louder than you would normally listen to meditation music as this series contains sound healing frequencies from the Acutonics Planetary Tuning Forks and Tibetan Singing Bowls and you want to be sure to get the full effect of the sound healing.

DO NOT LISTEN TO THESE CD's WHILE DRIVING.

Listen to each meditation in planetary order, starting with Mercury. Once you have listened to Mercury, it is best to pause the CD and go to the book to write down your impressions and visions. These will consist of whatever memories or thoughts that came to you while you were listening to the meditations. Then answer the questions that go with Mercury. Work with only one meditation at a time and be sure to follow the planetary order as the healing work will build and release as you work your way from Mercury to Sedna and the Sun. Take your time and really be honest with yourself as you write down your answers. The questions that don't make sense or seem to be a struggle are the ones that you need to answer the most.

Be diligent and persevere. The more you are honest and persevering, the more healing you will get out of this series. Open your heart and your mind and let the mythological planetary beings do their transformational work. Allow yourself to heal and become your most marvelous self. Take your time with each meditation and the corresponding book questions. Do only one or two meditations each day. Give yourself plenty of time to work through whatever may arise. This can be a truly life changing experience.

You can set the mood to do your meditations by choosing a time when you are least likely to be bothered. You may want to turn off the ringer on your telephone. Its best not be disturbed while you are doing this healing work. You may ask your family or roommates to respect your time while you are working on this series and hold all questions until you are ready to take them.

You may want to light some candles or burn some sage or other incense. Make yourself a comfortable place to lie down and relax as you listen to each meditation. You may want a warm blanket and some soft pillows. Take this opportunity to pamper yourself by indulging yourself in a comforting environment. Your body may feel heat or cold depending on what emotions you are working through. Sadness may release out of your body as a cold chill and frustration or anger may release as heat, feeling like a hot flash as the energy is moved out.

This series is designed to help you heal on the emotional and physical level. You may find that many old aches and pains are released out of the body over the course of this work. You may find that you are able to release many things and heal on many levels, if this is what you truly desire and are honest enough to do this healing work purposefully. You can use this series of meditations and the book again and again, for different trials that may arise in your life. This is a tool that you can utilize throughout your life whenever you feel you need some help working through certain issues in your life.

You may discover that the more you work with these meditations, the more intuitive and spiritual growth you may have. Several people have reported that their intuitive abilities seemed to be strengthened through the use of this series.

May you be blessed for your determination to heal as that is the catalyst that begins the process. May all your days be filled with light and promise. Know that you can make your life whatever you want it to be as long as you work toward the goal.

May your life be filled with Love and Joy,
    Michelle Marie Many

The Chakra System

The chakras are energy vortices that concentrate and swirl through the energy field that surrounds the body. These swirling concentrations of energy gather in specific areas of the body to fuel those energy systems of the body. The energy rises as it makes its way up the spine and pinwheels out from the front and back sides of the body as well as out the top of the head and out through your legs and feet. There are lesser chakras on the palms of the hands and the souls of the feet as well as behind the knees,

The first chakra sits at the base of the spine and shoots straight down into the earth and energizes the lower portion of the body and the legs and feet. This chakra spins in a red light frequency and grounds you through a strong connection to the earth and all of its beings. Through this energy vortex, you are connected to the tapestry of life and everything that lives on this planet.

The second chakra sits at the lower back and lower abdomen and energizes the pelvic region and all of its related organs. It is a place of passion and sensuality as well as emotion. This chakra spins in a pinwheel of orange light.

The third chakra sits at the solar plexus and fills us with yellow fire like the sun. This is the place where we decide what others might be thinking about us. Ego and matters of the self reside here. When in balance this chakra gives us the energy to be our most creative selves. It is the chakra that energizes our spleen and liver.

The fourth chakra sits at the heart and fills us with compassion and love when in balance. When out of balance, jealousy may arise. The energetic color frequency of the heart chakra can be pink when the love felt is conditional, however, it may be green if the love felt and emitted are unconditional. It can even be gold when the love is of a higher purpose. This kind of light shines like Jesus Christ's halo

The Chakra System, continued

and is very rarely found among our peers. This chakra energizes the lungs, heart, arms and hands.

The fifth chakra sits at the throat and spins in a blue light ray. This is the place of communication with our selves and others. It is a place of communication with our inner voice and our spirit guides and angels. It energizes the neck and shoulders, tonsils, thyroid and jaw.

The sixth chakra sits at the third eye center in the middle of the forehead and opens us to spirituality and divine grace. It is the place of the seeker of higher knowledge and higher purpose. It opens us to explore new kinds of spirituality. It is a place of psychic vision and intuition. It energizes the pineal gland, the brain, the medulla oblongata and the eyes and the ears. When shut down, it can cause severe depression and bipolar disorder. When in balance, it allows us to become our own guru and gives us the answers we are searching for.

The seventh chakra is pure white light that pours into us from the heavens, through the top of our head at the crown and showers us with cleansing divine energy. It is our connection to the heavens and divine inspiration. It is our connection to the realm of God.

There are several more chakras that sit above the body. The eighth chakra connects us with divine communication. The ninth chakra connects us with divine love. The tenth chakra pulls in divine knowledge. The eleventh chakra is our divine connection to all of our relations and ancestors. The twelfth chakra is the divine connection to our God. There are a total of twelve major chakras as well as the minor chakras and the Earth Star that connects us to this world which sits deep in Mother Earth.

This is only meant to be a quick study on the chakra system. You may want to do your own research on this subject.

Mercury The Winged Messenger

You are in a meadow in the Celtic lands of old. As you walk over a hillock through the tall green grass, you can hear the sounds of the evenings meadow at twilight and the birds are singing. As you come overthe top of the hill you can see a large bonfire in the distance with many people gathered around it. They are shouting and laughing. As you walk faster toward their fire, you can see that they are drinking from large mugs and splashing about the cool wine as they dance and sing. The place seems to be alive with activity as you approach the merry making. It seems to be a festival like the Celtic people used to have. It appears to be a Beltane festival.

Out of the backside of the fire comes the festival's Druidic High Priestess. She raises her hands over her head and the fire flashes higher. As the flames subside, you can see a large stag approaching the Beltane fire and the High Priestess. She stands royally, wearing a long white and gold robe and a headdress of fairy light. The large stag gets nearer. The others are dancing a river dance with quick steps as they tap and stomp their feet to the music. The stag reaches the High Priestess and she kisses his head between his long, branching antlers. He bows his head and kisses her hand. She turns from the fire and as she leaves with her stag, she says these words. "Speak only with love for each other and yourselves." He follows her into the forest. The others are singing loudly now and seem to be wishing the Priestess and her stag well, as they retreat to their forest bed.

You clap and stomp as you sing the fiery Beltane songs to the High Priestess and her stag. You feel the need to communicate to these people how wonderful they are making you feel as the joy of their festival fills your heart. The dance fills you with a sense of purpose and rhythm. The pounding steps of the dancer's dexterous feet seem to drum the rhythm of this planet into your body. Their eloquent songs fill your heart with joy and happiness. Your thoughts are rushing like a fast stream through your head. You are handed a large mug of wine and you take a long, heady drink. You can feel the

Mercury The Winged Messenger

warmth of the fire that rises from the back of your throat as you swallow the cool liquid.

Still alert, you see someone, a small yet well built man with silver sandels. His sandals have wings on the heels and you realize at once that this must be Hermes or Mercury himself, the winged messenger. He runs straight to you and hands you a paper scroll with a silver seal. You break the seal and open the scroll. The words are in a language that you understand as you read the paper. This message is specifically for you. Read it and memorize the words and their meaning. The meaning is just for you and applies to what you are currently learning in this moment in time. As you memorize the words and their meaning, you slip the scroll into your belt and thank Hermes for his message. You deposit some silver coins in his hand and he bows and runs in the opposite direction, no doubt headed to some other faraway land with an important message to deliver.

The night is growing quiet now as you find a place in the tall grass to rest. You lie back and look up at the night sky and all that it has to offer. You pull the light of the stars into your body and fill yourself with starlight. Your nervous system is calmed, as is your mind. You feel as if you understand all things with full knowledge. Your mind feels simultaneously alert and revitalized. You know that you have the choice to do that which will bring happiness and love to your life. You have the choice to speak with love to yourself and to those around you.

You stand up from your place in the grass and walk away from the Beltane fires, trusting yourself and your knowledge to do the right thing to create love in your life.

As you return to the room and your body, you feel a profound peace spread over you and only as soon as you are ready, you can go ahead and open your eyes.

Your Impression of Mercury

_____
_____
_____
_____
_____
_____
_____
_____
_____
_____
_____
_____
_____
_____
_____
_____
_____
_____
_____
_____
_____
_____
_____
_____
_____
_____
_____
_____
_____
_____

Mercury The Winged Messenger
Healing Questions

"...Speak only with love for each other and for yourselves..."
Druidic High Priestess

What message did Hermes' scroll reveal to you?_____
_____
_____
_____

What do you think this message means to you, and how does it relate
to your life?_____
_____
_____
_____
_____

How does Hermes' message relate to what you are currently learning
in this moment?_____
_____
_____
_____

What choices are available to you right now that will bring you more
happiness and love in your life? _____
_____
_____
_____

What could you do to increase your choices?_____
_____
_____
_____
_____

Mercury The Winged Messenger
Healing Questions

How did the Beltane festival make you feel?_____

_____

_____

_____

_____

In what ways are you allowing yourself to dance and feel the rhythms
of life? _____

_____

_____

_____

_____

What could you do to bring the rhythm and pulse back into your life
in any areas where it might be missing?_____

_____

_____

_____

_____

Extra Space For Answers

_____

_____

_____

_____

_____

_____

_____

_____

Venus The Bringer of Love

You are walking on the planet Venus. The soil is dark burgundy as are the trees and the bushes. There are burgundy mountains that are alive with volcanic activity and are spewing black sand. The sky and the clouds are shades of mauve and pinkish-purple hues. You see lovers dancing in a marble floored plaza with tall marble columns of pink and burgundy. The dancers are dressed in finery of laces and velvets. They are dancing a waltz. They seem to speak of harmony and beauty, refinement and sociability. You can feel their dance awakening those things within you.

As you continue walking the terrain of this lovely planet, you see lovers in clutching embraces with loving attention, appreciation and communication shining in their eyes as they look longingly at each other. As you continue on your walk, you find a forum with garnet pillars. A breeze blows gently across the forum as figures in Greco-Roman togas stand around discussing with great verve, what is just and fair. They seem to be discussing politics of some sort and cooperation seems to be the key to their resolve. Their voices ring with sensibility and the awareness of what is needed at this time. They speak of the power and potential of joyous relationships and remind you again, that cooperation is the key.

You continue walking until their voices are out of range. You round a corner in the garden landscape of this burgundy planet and find a beautiful bride in lace and old-fashioned organza. She is standing in a golden light with lilies in her hands. She seems to be awaiting her future husband. Her disposition is one of peace and certainty as she awaits her future love and his warm embrace that will take her forward in her lessons on love. As you gaze upon her, you can feel your heart chakra opening and emitting a beautiful light pink and light-green glow. The colors begin to spin at your chest and pinwheel out in a spiral of light.

She shows you a small green tree with fruits of pink and gold. She picks a pear shaped fruit from the tree and hands it to you. There are small bunnies running around the base of the tree. They are munching

Venus The Bringer of Love

on the leaves of the little tree. You take a bite of the sumptuous fruit and your mouth is filled with the sweet and tangy juice and the flesh of this marvelous pear. As the flavor of the fruit and its delicious juices run down your throat, you are at once happy and complete, satisfied and at peace with this world. You thank the bride for her gifts and as you get ready to leave the planet Venus, you feel the grace that has been bestowed upon your being, by the love that is emitted by this beautiful planet. You know that the more that you choose to walk your path with love, the happier and healthier you will be.

You have been given many gifts, it is up to you to use them where you can. Taking back with you all of the gifts of loving attention, appreciation, communication and beauty, as well as the last words of the bride; she said, "To love and be loved is the greatest thing that you will ever learn."

As you return to Earth and this room, you are full of love and know what it means to love and be loved. Whenever you are ready you can open your eyes now.

Your Impression of Venus

_____

_____

_____

_____

_____

_____

_____

_____

_____

_____

_____

_____

_____

_____

_____

_____

_____

_____

_____

_____

_____

_____

_____

_____

_____

_____

_____

_____

_____

_____

_____

_____

Venus The Bringer of Love
Healing Questions

"You see lovers in clutching embraces with loving attention, appreciation and communication shining in their eyes as they look longingly at each other"

How did the dancers and the lovers make you feel?_____

_____

_____

_____

In what ways could your cooperation be a key to the relationships in your life?_____

_____

_____

_____

_____

In what ways could you increase cooperation and appreciation in your relationships with others?_____

_____

_____

_____

_____

What love lessons are you currently learning?_____

_____

_____

_____

_____

_____

_____

Venus The Bringer of Love
Healing Questions

How will you be better as a person when you have learned these
lessons and how will your life change for the better?_____
_____
_____
_____

In what ways could you be walking your path with more love?_____
_____
_____
_____
_____
_____

In what ways are you currently loving and being loved?_____
_____
_____
_____
_____

What do you need to know that you are loved?_____
_____
_____
_____
_____

What words or gestures are important for you to know that someone
is being sincere with you?_____
_____
_____
_____

There is No Place Like Ohm

You are walking barefoot, up a shallow river; the sand in the river bottom is red. There are tall sandstone mesas that tower over the canyon floor where the river runs. The sky above is a piercing blue. As you walk up the red sandy river, you come to a sand bar. You can feel the texture of the sand beneath your feet and smell the fresh, clean water of the shallow river. You stop and as you stand on the sand bar, you shove your feet deep into the red sand. You can feel the red sand squish between your toes. The red Earth feels supportive and yet allowing as you shove your feet deeper into the cool, wet sand. You feel connected to your body and you can also feel your body's connection to the Earth through your feet. You are solid and capable in this place and you know that this place exists within you. You can call on the strength of Mother Earth for support whenever you need to.

The scene shifts and you are now in a grassy garden. The garden is well manicured and the grass, plants and trees are all a very vibrant shade of green that seem to be lit from within. You notice some crystals that are scattered about the garden and decide to collect a few of these stones. You pick up a clear quartz point that just fits in the palm of your hand. The second stone that you find is an amethyst point of a similar size. The third stone that you pick up is a lovely chunk of rose quartz. You put the three stones into your pocket.

You hear a voice asking you if you have found your crystals. You turn to see a man in a monk's robe who is in the garden with you. He introduces himself as Saint Francis, and you notice a robin that is perched on his shoulder. He tells you that the clear quartz is for focus and clarity, and with these rocks, come these gifts for you to own and become. The gift of the amethyst is to open you to the spiritual world and all of the magic that it holds, if you only open yourself to it. He tells you that the third stone, the rose quartz, is a stone of love and fills your heart with all of the love that you are unable to get by looking for it in others. He tells you to hold this stone close to your heart and let it heal all of your love issues. As you hold the stone to your chest, you can feel that your heart is filled With love for yourself and you no longer have to look without for love but can now begin to find that love within you.

There is No Place Like Ohm

He points out three small cups that have been set at your feet. The first cup is filled with birdseed. The second cup is filled with green tea and the third is filled with cooked white rice. St. Francis tells you that these cups and the stones are gifts to you from the Earth. They will connect you to the Earth, ground you, nourish you and give you what you need to heal. You thank St. Francis for his gifts and he tells you to be sure to use them wisely.

You take your gifts and suddenly, space begins to fold in on itself and time is folding back on itself as you go farther out by folding within. Your body becomes heavy and solid. Transformed by the gifts of St. Francis and the Earth, your feet, ankles, knees, hips and low back are released from all old discomforts, as the solidity of the Earth becomes part of your body. You feel the power of Mother Earth energizing your entire body and making you whole in all of the places that you need it. The Earth is your home at this time and cradles you in its majesty. The Earth provides all of the things that you need to survive.

Thank Mother Earth for all of her support and her wonderful gifts of nature. Mother Earth gifts you with the ability to be comfortable in your body and to do whatever homework is necessary to become so. She gives you the balance needed to complete your destiny successfully. As you reenter the room you can feel the bottoms of your feet tingling as they remind you of your connection to the Great Mother.

You can open your eyes as soon as you are ready and when you do, place your feet against the ground and feel the power of Mother Earth rise up through the souls of your feet and through your legs into your torso, to fill your whole body with Earth energy. You are a being of the Earth so claim your power as such.

Your Impression of Earth

_____

_____

_____

_____

_____

_____

_____

_____

_____

_____

_____

_____

_____

_____

_____

_____

_____

_____

_____

_____

_____

_____

_____

_____

_____

_____

_____

_____

_____

_____

The Earth, No Place Like Om
Healing Questions

" ...You are solid and capable in this place and you know that this place exists within you...."

Clear Quartz - Focus - On what do you need to focus in your life for forward movement in love and joy? _____

_____

_____

_____

_____

_____

Amethyst - Spiritual Openings - To what facet of spirituality are you, or could you, be most open to exploring? _____

_____

_____

Rose Quartz - Love - In what ways are you looking for love by asking others to fulfill your needs? _____

_____

_____

In what ways do you feel unsupported in your life? _____

_____

_____

In what ways have you created that non-support? _____

_____

_____

How could you create a more supportive environment for yourself?

_____

_____

_____

_____

The Moon Fairy

You are walking through a meadow under the moonlight. Your footsteps are only very lightly touching the ground. You look up at the Moon above you, in wonder. As you stare at this beautiful body of light, you feel yourself being pulled up into the air and away from the ground. You are flying through the air, heading out of the atmosphere. As you break through the atmosphere, you can feel yourself slow down and begin to float. You are floating in outer space now. Ahead, you can see a small dark planet. You are being pulled toward the little planet. You notice a greenish-yellow ball of light approaching you that seems to have come from the backside of the little planet. As the ball of light draws nearer, you can see that the light is actually a small greenish-yellow fairy whose little being is filled with light. Her long, wavy hair, eyes and dress are all of this same color of greenish-yellow light. She pulls you around her moon by your head and draws you into an orbital pattern. You are orbiting this small moon as you follow in tow by the little fairy's light.

She tells you of the cycles of the moon and how the moon affects all the tides, in all of the water beings of the earth. As she pulls you along in orbit around her moon, she speaks to you of healing all of the things that cycle and wave through your life. She asks you if there is anything that you would like her to heal for you. She is very good at healing and nurturing and gives you whatever you need, be it physical or emotional. She pulls you down onto her planet and dunks you in a lake of greenish-yellow light. The water is dark, but the water seems to light your body with a greenish-yellow glow. The fairy is splashing you with the water and telling you to honor the feminine within. The water seems to bring a sort of psychic vision to your mind and allows you to see all of the things that you would like to change right now. Your instinct tells you to let go and allow change to happen magically.

You can feel your inner emotions swirling as the fairy swirls you through her dark waters of light. You feel perfectly secure in her little hands. She comes right up to your face and laughs her lilting fairy laugh as though she is having great fun. She takes some of her light

The Moon Fairy

and rolls it into a ball and she places it in your hand. She tells you that you can keep this bit of moonlight inside of you and she tells you to place it in your forehead. You can feel your intuitive powers expanding.

Suddenly, she pushes you on the forehead with both of her little hands and sends you sailing back to Earth. You fly backward and land with your feet lightly touching the meadow grass once again. As you walk through the meadow under the moon, you now feel connected to your Fairy Moon Goddess and know that her gift of moonlight is something that you can treasure forever. Your little fairy is always there for you to visit whenever you need to get the cycles in your life balanced. She brings balance in all things.

You can feel all the waters in your body balancing with her gift. All edemas flush out and all inflammations are released now. You can feel your body regulating all of the blood, synovial fluids, spinal fluid and any other fluid that moves through your body becomes balanced now.

As you return to the room, know that your little fairy walks with you and you can fly to the Moon whenever you wish. Open your eyes whenever you are ready and know that your fairy's gift of her little ball of moonlight lives just behind your eyes.

Your Impression of The Moon

_____
_____
_____
_____
_____
_____
_____
_____
_____
_____
_____
_____
_____
_____
_____
_____
_____
_____
_____
_____
_____
_____
_____
_____
_____
_____
_____
_____

The Moon Fairy
Healing Questions

"The ball of light draws nearer; you can see that the light is actually a small greenish-yellow fairy whose little being is filled with light"

What did you ask the fairy to heal for you?_____
_____
_____

What did you see with your psychic vision that you would like to change about yourself or your life?_____
_____
_____
_____

What can you do, starting right now, that will begin to bring about that wanted change? _____
_____
_____

What things need to be flushed out of you or your life for healing to take place? _____
_____
_____
_____

What things are cycling through your life that are asking you to heal and let go of old, repeating patterns that no longer serve you?
_____
_____
_____

What patterns need reweaving to return your heart to love?_____
_____
_____
_____

Mars The Warrior

You are on the deck of a huge sailing vessel. You see a warrior dressed in full battle dress. The wind blows through his shoulder-length, brown wavy hair as he gazes at the horizon. You can see an island up ahead. The island is burning. Its city is alight with immense flames that are shooting up into the night sky from the little island in the sea. As you watch the warrior, you can see his anguish as his heart leaps in his chest. He looks on with great distress as the fleeting moments rush by. His great ship slowly approaches the island. He calls for a rowboat and hops in, as the boat is lowered into the water, over the side of his great ship. The rowboat is only big enough for about twenty people and you and the warrior are both wondering how many he will be able to save. He rows toward the shore as though he is in a race. He races against time and the brutal ravages of the quickening flames.

Once on the shore, he quickly pulls the rowboat up on the sand and shoves it under a palm tree for safekeeping. He runs full speed into the burning city. Amidst the shouts and screams of terror and loss, he searches for his home and his family. You look on as many of the buildings are burning with thick flames and menacing smoke that is billowing from the doorways and windows.

At last, you see the warrior come to the building that he recognizes as his family home. The door is swung wide and you can hear the sounds of the children and their nanny searching for safety in the midst of the burning ruins of what used to be their happy home. The nanny is yelling the names of the children. The warrior runs to his bedroom and out the bedroom patio door. He finds his wife sitting in a large, white wicker chair on the veranda. She is crying. He scoops her up into his big strong arms and tells her softly that they must go. He runs with her in his arms to the kitchen area where, only moments ago, he heard the sound of the nanny's voice calling to his children.

As he enters, he sees the nanny with his three children huddled around her. He tells her that they must leave right now. She says that they will follow him. He runs out of the door with his wife in his arms

Mars The Warrior

and his nanny and children in tow and they run down the narrow little street. They find the nanny's husband and son who were on their way to find her. The warrior tells them to follow him and they head for the beach.

At the beach, the warrior sees his father talking to his wife's parents. His wife's sister is with them. They spot him and come running. He also sees his brother's family coming from the opposite direction. You can feel the relief emanating from the warrior as he realizes that he has most of his family safe and sound around him on the beach. After much hugging and crying, the warrior gathers everyone into the small rowboat. He grabs a few children who are standing alone and crying. They tell him that they can't find their parents. They tell him that their mommy and daddy never came home. Grandma went out to look for them and she didn't come back, so they ran to the beach to their favorite spot, where they usually come to play. They pointed to the palm tree under which only moments earlier the rowboat had been parked. He puts the children on to the rowboat with his family and they head back to the ship.

They reach the ship and are all safely put aboard. They stand along the ship's rail and watch their beautiful island city burn. They are safe for the rescue but sad for the loss. The warrior, now Captain, addresses his new passengers and tells them that he will sail them in new directions to visit exciting new lands and have wonderful new opportunities to make new fortunes. Everyone cheers and their hearts are gladdened, as is yours. They have come through the fire and let go of all of those things that no longer serve them, no matter how much they thought they needed them. They are lighter and better for having purged with fire all those things that they had been dragging around with them that were unnecessary and burdensome. They tell you to give your burdens to their burning city and let the fire clear away all those things that you no longer need. You feel the release as your burdens are magically lifted off of your shoulders and are purged by the flames of the burning city.

Mars The Warrior

You can feel your energy shift with the release. You note the courage and incredible fortitude of these people as they ready themselves for new horizons. You realize that your headings can be tweaked to a much happier setting with much more ease than what these folks have to bear. You realize that you can sail your own personal vessel with as much speed and new direction as you are ready for. You can set your headings for love and joy with strength and confidence. You head into your new horizons with courage and determination. Your resolve is powerful. You can do whatever you really desire to do. It is simply a matter of where you set your directional compass and where you put your energy into going. The more energy you put into where you want to go, the better chance you have of not only getting there but also getting there faster and more efficiently.

So right now, put your energies into where you want to go the most and create that reality for yourself. No one else is going to create your reality for you. So decide where you really want to be in life and set your compass heading for smooth sailing, as you head for calm seas. As you feel your direction changing and becoming more focused, you can feel your own personal sailing ship begin to run full speed ahead as you trim the sails to define your own joy.

When you have your headings set, and you can feel your ship sailing full speed ahead. Let yourself sail with the wind in your hair and know that you have set a course for new directions for love and happiness.

Only as soon as you are ready, you can sail back into the room, into your body and only as soon as you can, you may go ahead and open your eyes.

Your Impression of Mars

_____

_____

_____

_____

_____

_____

_____

_____

_____

_____

_____

_____

_____

_____

_____

_____

_____

_____

_____

_____

_____

_____

_____

_____

_____

Mars The Warrior
Healing Questions

...They tell you to give your burdens to their burning city and let the fire clear away all of those things that you no longer need. You feel the release as your burdens are magically lifted off of your shoulders and are purged by the flames of the burning city...

What things in your life have become burdensome and unnecessary?

_____
_____
_____
_____

What needs to be tossed into the fire and released for you to heal?

_____
_____
_____
_____
_____

In what direction do you need to set your sails for smoother sailing?

_____
_____
_____
_____
_____

In what new ways could you be expressing yourself to create more joy in your life? _____

_____
_____
_____
_____
_____

Mars The Warrior
Healing Questions

Where do you need to take responsibility for your creations and be the strong warrior who fights courageously, for what he/she believes in and stands firm in those convictions and the world that he/she has created? _____

_____

_____

_____

_____

What have you been capable of surviving, and how has it made you stronger as a person? _____

_____

_____

_____

_____

_____

_____

Extra Space For Answers

_____

_____

_____

_____

_____

_____

_____

_____

_____

_____

_____

_____

_____

_____

Jupiter The Emperor

You are on the planet Jupiter. You can see a palace in the distance. As you approach the palace, you can see its smooth dome silhouetted against the purple clouds of the darkening twilight sky. You enter the palace and are escorted to the throne room. You enter a large hall with a long purple rug with gold edging. The rug leads to a large throne. The throne is made of Sapphire. A large muscular man with a head of thick, curly silver hair sits upon the throne. On his head, neatly nestled in his silver locks, sits a crown of silver that is embellished with sapphires and lapis lazuli. The man seems distraught. He is watching a scene play out before him in miniature. The scene shows something that is taking place in the realm of the mortals.

He is Jupiter or Zeus and is the ruler of the immortals as well as the mortals. The God of the Gods, his home is Mt. Olympus, and his throne and palace are located there. He lets out a sigh that is really more of a grumble. He claps his hands near his head and the scene in front of him disappears. Jupiter's dismay however, does not. The emperor sits with his head resting on his fist and contemplates what to do about the chaos that exists in the mortal world. He walks between worlds, and you follow him as he goes to the land of the mortals to heal the chaos. He becomes so distraught with the dramas that he encounters that in anger, he reacts. He sees the indulgences and pride of mortal man. He is having trouble finding wisdom and understanding for such gluttony. Jupiter sends rain and storms to clear the land and the excesses of mortal men from the Earth realm. Jupiter returns to his throne to think things through before he reacts again in anger.

As he sits on his throne once again, we see Jupiter forming plans to resolve the chaos with logic rather than anger. He is a great battle chief and knows how to strategize a proper and respectful resolution to the chaos of the mortal realm. He is able to see the big picture from his throne and he understands that a wise ruler must lead through tolerance. He knows that true knowledge comes through understanding. You can feel yourself expanding and opening to the optimism of growth and success as you are filled with the power of Jupiter and his home

Jupiter The Emperor

of the immortal Gods of Mt. Olympus, where he rules with optimism and enthusiasm for the mortal world. He knows that mortal man is learning through social consciousness, what is moral and ethical. As well as what brings success and achievement, even abundance and opulence when well met.

Jupiter's gift to you is the power to stimulate growth and expansion on all levels and break the illusory boundaries between spirit and matter. You can feel this growth happening in every cell in your being, expanding your consciousness on all levels and opening you to prosperity and luck. Breathe deeply and take this gift deep into your body and soul. Know that you are fearless and strong, a warrior of the new day. Hold the big picture in your mind and all that it brings to you in the way of choices and new opportunities for reaching far horizons. Allow yourself to step into new ways of expressing yourself and new ways of thinking. With new choices come new possibilities and ways of doing things that are more efficient and productive. Jupiter, with his new plan in place, watches as the chaos resolves almost immediately. Jupiter sits once again on his throne, ruling the Gods with tolerance and true knowledge from the heart. Know that you can rule your own world that you have created, in the same way.

With love, all things are possible in this world and the next. Say thank you to the emperor for his gifts of understanding and wisdom and return to the Earth and this room. Only as quickly as you can and only as soon as you are ready, you may open your eyes.

Your Impression of Jupiter

Jupiter The Emperor
Healing Questions

...You can feel yourself expanding and opening to the optimism of growth and success as you are filled with the power of Jupiter and his home of the immortal Gods of Mt. Olympus, where he rules with optimism and enthusiasm for the mortal world....

In what ways could you resolve the chaos in your world with logic rather than anger? _____
_____
_____
_____
_____
_____
_____

In what areas of your life do you need to be more proper and respectful in working through a strategy for your resolutions of chaos? _____
_____
_____
_____
_____
_____

In what ways could tolerance and understanding bring growth and even success to your life? _____
_____
_____
_____
_____
_____
_____

Jupiter The Emperor
Healing Questions

What new choices could expand your growth and success if you were fearless enough to embrace them? _____

_____

_____

_____

_____

_____

Where in your life do you need more efficient and productive ways of doing things?_____

_____

_____

_____

_____

_____

What could you do to be more efficient and productive in these areas of your life, starting right now? _____

_____

_____

_____

_____

_____

_____

_____

_____

_____

Saturn The Golden Age

You are walking through a lush landscape that is similar to what you might see in a place like Yellowstone National Park. You are walking through a lush green meadow filled with sweet-smelling flowers of all colors. There are tall pine trees, and the sky is as bright blue as a robin's egg. You are visiting the myth of the planet Saturn. You hear a moose bellow in the distance. There are little squirrels running back and forth between your feet, hopping through the tall grass of the meadow. You look up and see an eagle overhead with an amazingly huge wingspan that is darkly contrasted against the bright blue sky. You can feel the laws of nature at work here. The achievement of nature through time is profound. A family of deer cautiously prance along a narrow trail that winds through the trees near you. They see you but persevere along their course. Their perseverance becomes yours. You notice that the squirrels are gathering their winter stores and shoving them into the nearest trees. They are very busy and are working very hard at their task. Their self-discipline is a wonderful thing to watch, and you take some their disciplinary energy with you as you continue walking along.

As you are walking through the tall grass, you see a large bear walking a few hundred feet away. He hasn't noticed you so you take a good long look at his powerful body and sigh deeply at his majesty. You breathe deep and pull his power into you. With caution, you step behind a tree until he passes. The wind is blowing the other way and his nose is involved with another smell so he didn't notice you at all. You follow a grassy path along a stream. It leads you down into a valley. The stream ends at a large, gushing waterfall of magnificent height. You stand under it and are at once consumed and cleansed by its rushing waters. You step out of the fall, feeling clear and cleansed. You see a moose and an elk standing side-by-side, drinking from the waters of the stream. This place seems timeless and beyond time. It is very old and very mature, yet it is bursting with new life. Generations and regenerations of life.

You follow the path and it leads up out of the valley to a plateau.

Saturn The Golden Age

You see a geyser spouting in the distance. As you approach the spouting geyser, you see that it is Old Faithful in all her magnificence. She spouts forth an angelic stream of steam and water; her magnificent wings extending fully. She reminds you once again of what can be achieved though power and the stability and structure found in the timeless strengths of nature.

You lie down in a small grassy meadow and begin to dream. You are spending a lazy summer afternoon by the lake. It is Fourth of July, and your family is at their summer cabin having a barbecue by the lake. You can smell hot dogs and hamburgers on the grill. Grandma is bringing her famous apple pie out on the porch and putting it on the picnic table as she admonishes Dad for trying to put a finger in her freshly baked pie.

There are baskets of fuchsias hanging on the porch and you are nestled in a porch swing with a warm breeze blowing through your hair. You can hear the kids at the cabin next door shouting out to passers by that they have fresh lemonade for sale, for only a quarter a glass.

The sun is setting now and you can hear the sounds of the grandpa's power tools in the garage and the smell of saw dust as he puts together a lovely birdhouse for the backyard. You can hear the younger children playing hide and seek. You hear Mom telling them to come in now. You are dozing on the porch swing.

As you nap you feel your body filling with all of the gifts of Saturn. You are timeless and protected in this place. You are at once aware of your own powers of solidity, self-knowledge, self-control and self-awareness. You understand your own boundaries and are capable of setting them with solidity and self-control. You are capable of achieving whatever you desire with a true heart and can manifest whatever you need as long your heart and integrity are in place. You are at once appreciative of your powers of survival and strength. You can feel your solar plexus expanding and emitting a strong and powerful yellow flame. You can feel your root open and connect to the timelessness of this planet through your legs and feet, spreading outward and connecting with the web of life. You are as solid as a granite cliff and as capable as the eagle that soars over your head. Let those strengths and capabilities awaken in you now. Let that self-knowledge and self-awareness, be yours now. Let your powers of self-control and self-trust guide you to set boundaries with confidence that you will do what is best for you.

With these gifts in place, only as soon as you are ready, you may return to the room and open your eyes.

Your Impression of Saturn

_____
_____
_____
_____
_____
_____
_____
_____
_____
_____
_____
_____
_____
_____
_____
_____
_____
_____
_____
_____
_____
_____
_____
_____
_____
_____
_____

Saturn The Golden Age
Healing Questions

"You can feel the laws of nature at work here. The achievement of nature through time is profound"

Where do you need more perseverance and self-control in your life?

_____
_____
_____
_____
_____

What could you achieve with more perseverance and self-control in these areas? _____

_____
_____
_____
_____

What parameters need to be set in your life to allow you to heal and bring you more joy and success? _____

_____
_____
_____
_____

In what areas of your life could you be more trusting of your own strengths and capabilities, and how would that self-trust resolve issues and release unnecessary fears? _____

_____
_____
_____
_____

Saturn and The Golden Age
Healing Questions

What are your biggest trust issues, and where do they come from?

_____
_____
_____
_____
_____
_____
_____

How does this serve you now? _____
_____
_____
_____
_____

How does this limit you? _____
_____
_____
_____
_____
_____

How else could this service be rendered that is more productive?

_____
_____
_____
_____
_____
_____
_____
_____

Chiron The Wounded Healer

You are flying in a cosmic craft through outer space. Your personal spacecraft is flying around a small planetary body between Saturn and Uranus that is being held in check by the gravitational pulls of the great planets. You are heading around the backside of the little planetary body that is known as a Centaur. This Centaur is known as Chiron, the wounded healer. You can see low, spreading, greenish-black volcanoes that are spewing greenish-red and black lava. The lava seems to be thicker and slower than normal Earth flows. You follow around the planet in your little craft until you are on the front side of the planetary body. It looks like a dark jungle that is lit by a pink-gold sun.

A large man with lots of muscle is coming toward your craft, which you have just landed in the midst of Chiron's dark jungle growth. The man is approaching your craft at a good clip. He looks like a Greek God with a stallion's rear end. In his front leg is a large bone stake. It is shoved deeply into his leg and has created a large irregular shaping of flesh around the wound. He introduces himself to you as Chiron, the wounded healer. You ask him about the stake in his leg and he explains that the stake keeps the wound's poison from spreading throughout his body and contains the wound. He reminds you that he is here to heal you and not the other way around.

You are humbled in the presence of the greatest healer. He asks you to lie down in the grass and he begins to work on you with a big knife. He works his knife in between the vertebras of your spine, realigning the discs and opening the disc spaces as needed, in all of the places in your spine that need work. He works through the cervical vertebrae of your neck. He places little pieces of moldavite crystals into the areas of your spine that need healing. Next he takes his knife and uses it to move the sacral and pelvic bones into right relationship with each other and frees your hips of any discomfort that you may have been having lately. He places a large piece of dark opalescent labradorite into the sacral bone and tells you that

Chiron The Wounded Healer

it will keep your lower back strong and healthy. Your spine, neck and low back instantly feel supported and strengthened. He sticks a few more gemstones of moldavite and labradorite into places in your body that need healing. He places a clear quartz over your third eye, on your forehead and blows light into the crystal. It lights up and so does your head. You can feel yourself filling with light from your forehead, and that light is spreading down through your whole body.

He places a few more stones around your heart and abdomen area and then he gives your leg a good tug. Your hips shake and the stones fall into you and you feel the stones jostle themselves into exactly the right places for healing to take place in your body. He pushes a large piece of green moldavite, the size of a baseball, into your heart chakra.

His planet suddenly changes and begins to look like a Hawaiian Island, tropical and lush. You can see and smell beautiful tropical flowers in big blooms of bright oranges and reds. You feel renewed, as if old baggage from the ages has been set free from your personal cargo bay. A large bear approaches you and Chiron. Chiron pets the bear and he growls softly. Chiron tells you that the bear is speaking of stability, solidity and inner knowledge. Chiron says that the bear is here to heal you of your mistrust and sorrow. The bear walks up to where you are lying, and he lies down beside you. You can feel his warm body and his soft fur as he nudges up against you. He lies beside you and snores for some time. You wonder how this is healing you. You laugh to yourself and enjoy the warmth and soothing snoring of the big bear. Finally, the bear rises and slowly walks away. Chiron thanks him as he leaves, and so do you.

Chiron asks you how you are feeling and helps you to stand up. As you stand, you notice that you feel incredibly strong and vibrant. Chiron looks at you with compassion and tells you that you now have the wisdom to grow and learn to become your most marvelous self,

Chiron The Wounded Healer

as this was the gift from the bear. You can feel the truth of this in every cell of your being. You thank Chiron for all of his good healing work as you say goodbye to him and return once again to your personal spacecraft. You fly away from the Centaur and back into outer space. As you head toward Earth, you think of all of the wonderful healing that has just taken place and how strong and solid you feel.

Your ship returns you to Earth and to this room as you return to your body. You feel solid and happy as you open your eyes, only as quickly as you can and only as soon as your ready.

Your Impression of Chiron

_____
_____
_____
_____
_____
_____
_____
_____
_____
_____
_____
_____
_____
_____
_____
_____
_____
_____
_____
_____
_____
_____
_____
_____
_____
_____
_____
_____
_____
_____
_____
_____

Chiron The Wounded Healer
Healing Questions

...You are humbled in the presence of the greatest healer.
He asks you to lie down in the grass, and he begins to work on you...

Where in your spine and hips did you feel healing taking place?
_____
_____

What else in your body was healed by Chiron? _____
_____

In what ways did Chiron's snoring bear heal you? _____
_____
_____
_____
_____

Where could you integrate more stability and solidity into your life?
_____
_____
_____
_____

What areas of your life need improvement?_____
_____
_____
_____
_____

What could you do, starting right now, to begin to make those
improvements? _____
_____
_____
_____

Chiron The Wounded Healer
Healing Questions

What one thing could you commit to, right now, that would begin to improve your life? _____

_____

In what ways might you be sabotaging your self from success in your life and in your relationships? _____

_____

_____

Where does this fear come from that creates the sabotage? _____

_____

_____

_____

Is this fear relevant today? _____

Does this still protect you in a productive way? _____

Would you rather be free of it? _____

One way to release this is to write the fear on a stone and throw the stone as far from you as you can, into a stream or a field with the intent of releasing this fear. Another way, is to carve into a candle, the fear issue and the names of any people who are connected to this fear. Then light the candle and as it burns imagine yourself being freed from this fear forever.

Are you allowing yourself to create and grow, to become your most magnificent self? _____

_____

What do you truly need within yourself to be whole?_____

_____

_____

58

Uranus The Sky God

You are walking through a beautiful green forest of tall pine trees. As you hike, the ground begins to rise beneath your feet as you follow a path up a hillside to the top of the hill where there is a large clearing. You lie down on the soft grassy floor of the forest and look up at the sky. The clouds above you are laid out in lines that are spreading apart into a sort of fabric. The fabric of the sky. You imagine yourself lying on the fabric of clouds and can feel the softness of the pillowy clouds under your back. The clouds begin to move you through the heavens. As you travel out into the heavens, you can see the planets swirling in the night sky. You are aware of the planets growing larger as your view seems to take you closer to the heavenly bodies of our solar system. You are deep in outer space now with the planets moving around you like great ships on a plotted course.

Off in the distance, you can see the Sky God, Uranus. He is a regal man with a thick chest and strong legs that are encircled around heavy calves, by leather thongs that attach to his sandals. His attire is simple but his presence is commanding. He wears a long robe of sky-blue with cloud-white trim. He is sitting on a planet, the planet Uranus, as though it were his throne. The throne of the Sky God. With a wave of his hand, the sun flares into a long finger-like spike and then shrinks back to a more circular sphere. He shakes his head, and thunder cracks loudly over a grassy field on Earth. The thunder is followed by a lightning bolt that lights up the field like stadium lights at a night game. The rain begins to fall on the grassy field. The Sky God is pacing between the planets, causing shifts in the axis and rotations of the affected planets. He sits down hard on his throne, on the planet Uranus and the planet rolls so that its axis is nearly horizontal. He swirls a wand as though twirling water in a pond with a stick. A comet flashes out of the end of the wand and swirls in a spiral pattern like a stick breaking the surface of a pond and causing ripples.

The Sky God stands on his planet and conducts the solar system like a conductor would a symphony. He inspires genius and creativity at its highest level. He is rebellious and original in his expressions of

Uranus The Sky God

self. He tosses out stormy seas and disrupts the doldrums. He brings about rapid and explosive changes that are needed in your life and you feel these changes shift your world. You are at once inspired to initiate changes in your life wherever necessary, throwing out old patterns and habits that aren't productive and healthy, in favor of the new and unusual. Uranus, the Sky God throws us into unexpected and unknown places to experience and learn what we need to know to advance on our paths, expanding our field of awareness.

You can feel yourself growing calm and relaxed as all tension is released out of your lower body. You can feel the kundalini flow rising in your spine, moving energy upward and filling you with electricity and revitalizing all of the systems in your body. You can feel yourself commanding your body to a healthy balance, the way the Sky God commands his planets. You send energy like comets, shooting to all of the places in your body that need energy and healing. You realize your own resourcefulness and powers of innovation as you move through the world of your body, setting things right and making changes that are needed.

As you feel the energy shifting through your body, you can feel yourself healing at all levels. Take a deep breath and pull the energy of the planets deep into your body. Let it light up your chakric energy centers like stars, each one shining brightly in its own color. The red star shines through your hips, down your legs and into your feet. The orange star lights up your abdomen and lower back. The yellow star fills your lower chest and mid-back. The green star lights up your heart and upper back. The blue star shines at your throat, and the purple star lights up your forehead at the third eye center. The top of your head shines with bright white starlight that spins light in from the heavens. Your body is filled with the light of the colors of the chakric stars.

You are a star in the heavens, creating your own world. From your new perspective of the world of the Sky God, you can see how easy it

Uranus The Sky God

is to create what you want and need in your life. You realize that you have been ruling your world all along, although mostly unconsciously. Now with new awareness, you can create what you need to learn from in an easier and more productive way. Everything that has happened to you in your life has been an unconscious choice. Now you can consciously make choices to learn and better yourself in more comfortable ways. If you aren't happy with what you have currently chosen to learn from, or the way that you have chosen to learn, you can change that now. You can still learn the lesson with conscious choices for change instead of learning through the whims of what your unconscious decides might work.

As you allow yourself to believe that you are the ruler of your world, you realize that if you don't like what you have created, only you can change it. Be your own Sky God, and rule your world with love and kindness for yourself and everyone in your world. Make it a happy place to be. Feel the resolve flow over your body like a wave of consciousness, that you will create a joyous world for yourself starting right now.

Take a deep breath and feel those changes locking in now. Let your new star-like self return to Earth with all of the gifts of Uranus. As you return to the room and into your body, feeling fully relaxed, and at the same time, revitalized by all of the positive changes that you have just made and will continue to make in your world. Only as soon as you can, go ahead and open your eyes.

Your Impression of Uranus

_____
_____
_____
_____
_____
_____
_____
_____
_____
_____
_____
_____
_____
_____
_____
_____
_____
_____
_____
_____
_____
_____
_____
_____
_____
_____
_____
_____

Uranus The Sky God
Healing Questions

"The Sky God stands on his planet and conducts the solar system like a conductor would a symphony. He inspires genius and creativity at its highest level"

In what positive ways are you original in your self-expression? _____
_____
_____

In what ways do you rely on old patterns because they feel safe even when they no longer serve you? _____
_____
_____
_____
_____

Where in your life do you need to make dramatic changes to set things on the right track for yourself and those around you? _____
_____
_____
_____

Where in your life are you ready to throw out old patterns and habits that aren't productive or healthy, in favor of the new and unusual? __
_____
_____
_____

Where do you need to expand your horizons to be able to advance on your path? _____
_____
_____
_____

The Dolphins of Neptune

You are swimming in crystal blue-green waters. There are dolphins swimming with you. The dolphins are laughing and jumping high out of the water. The sky is a light fuchsia shade. The dolphins rise up out of the water as it streams down their smooth backs. The bellies of the dolphins are the color of the water, a beautiful turquoise-green. Their backs are the color of the sky in soft tones of fuchsia and pink. The dolphins glide along the surface of the water and circle around you. One of them comes underneath you and you feel his back lift you up above the surface of the water and carry you along in the turquoise waves that are created as the dolphin moves you through the water.

The wind is soft and light and kisses your cheeks as the dolphins continue to play with you. They take you to a fairy grotto. The grotto is covered in ferns and dripping with fresh water that falls in a light sprinkle into the ocean waters. There are several little fairies playing on the surface of the water and in the waterfall. Each time they light on the surface of the water, a flower blooms underneath them. They are making flower chains and are pulling each other around by the flower chains and laughing in high tinkly voices.

The landscape of the planet Neptune that surrounds this vast turquoise-green sea are lowlands of waving mint-green grassy-like ground cover. The mountains shoot up almost from sea level and are a darker shade of the same turquoise-green as the water. The mountains are covered in pink and purple snow. One of the mountains is erupting like a great aquamarine jewel spouting pink snow.

You are still relaxing in the cool water and feeling refreshed. The dolphins and fairies fill your heart with joy. You can hear music that sounds like angles singing. Frolicking with the dolphins and fairies of Neptune is a mystical experience that transcends mind, body and spirit. You are totally relaxed and at peace as you float in the healing waters of Neptune's sea. You ask your body to remember this feeling of complete serenity. You feel yourself sinking deeper into your inner space ocean of consciousness. You feel your very DNA re-encoding

The Dolphins of Neptune

to a higher reality as your yearning for the infinite is fulfilled by the healing waters of Neptune's sea. You can feel deception and illusion being washed away. Your vision becomes focused and clear as you strive for expression outside of your normal parameters. Neptune's magic takes you back to a preexisting state and seeks to help you connect with the collective feeling of universal love.

As you become more visionary, you understand the need for unity that is caused by separation from the universal heart. You are opened to the mystery of your spiritual urges. You feel yourself escaping the limitations of normal reality and the dreamer becomes the dissolver as outdated patterns and attachments are dissolved, making room for new growth. Lost power is reclaimed in this place as you are allowed to access your potential for intuitive growth, imagination and creative awareness. The frequency of this planet opens you to cosmic awareness as you become the psychic and the prophet of your own journey. All mysterious pain is released now from all the areas in your body that are affected. Your nervous system is at once calmed and nurtured.

As you are nurtured by the magic of the planet Neptune, you can feel your spinal column and feet line up into one continuous stream that is fed by the waters of the spinal fluid. The spinal fluid is brought into a subtle rhythmic flow by the waters of Neptune's sea. As you feel your body rocked by the waves and motion of the waters of the ocean of Neptune, all things are readjusted in the flow. All things return to rightness and are re-patterned from this place. The illusive healing qualities of this planet and its waters wash you with imagination for what could be in your life if you take the time to create it.

You climb out of the water and lie on the turquoise sand of the Neptunian shore. You see a big seashell lying near you so you reach over and pick it up. Inside of the huge shell is a platinum circlet with aquamarines and turquoise gems set into it. You place it on your head and it slides down over your forehead and rests there with the

The Dolphins of Neptune

biggest aquamarine sitting right at your third eye. You hear someone laughing and see a group of mermaids splashing in the water near the shore. They are inviting you to play. They remind you how important it is to play and have fun. They are creating spiral patterns with their bodies as they glide through the water. They are the epitome of creativity and bliss, and they give this to you as a gift. They come to you and each one gives you a big hug and a kiss on the cheek and places a flower in your hand or in your hair. Each mermaid has a special word that she whispers in your ear. Pay attention and remember each word that is given to you by the mermaids, as they are powerful affirmations for you. Their long hair tangles around them as they swirl themselves through the water around you. They swim you up the coastline to an underwater cave. They pull you under the water and into the cave.

As you emerge above the water line inside of the cave, you see that the cave is lined with aquamarine gemstones. There is a small beach of turquoise sand. You climb out onto the sand and see that the sand is strewn with aquamarines, blue topaz and turquoise. You lie there feeling the power of these gems fill your body with bluish-green light. It is like an anesthetic and you feel a bit intoxicated as you lie on the turquoise sand among the gemstones. You feel your mind, body, soul and spirit healing on all levels as you lie in this blue grotto, on this blue planet. You take in the frequency of Neptune and vow to keep this feeling in your memory - in the memory of your mind and body so that you can access this feeling at any time and remember it emotionally, spiritually and neurologically. You feel one of the mermaids tap your forehead three times, just above the aquamarine stone in the circlet of platinum that you are wearing. As she taps your forehead, you feel your body and soul remembering this experience on a very deep level that can be accessed whenever you desire to be on the planet Neptune or in the healing waters of the Neptunian Sea.

Bringing all these wonderful gifts, words and memories back with you, you can now return to the room. As soon as you're ready, go ahead and open your eyes.

Your Impression of Neptune

_____
_____
_____
_____
_____
_____
_____
_____
_____
_____
_____
_____
_____
_____
_____
_____
_____
_____
_____
_____
_____
_____
_____
_____
_____
_____
_____
_____

The Dolphins of Neptune
Healing Questions

"Frolicking with the dolphins and fairies of Neptune is a mystical experience that transcends mind, body and spirit"

Where in your life do you need to wash away deception and illusions?

_____

_____

_____

How have you recently experienced intuitive growth? _____

_____

_____

How could you better use your imagination and creative awareness?

_____

_____

_____

What message did the mermaids have for you, and how can you apply it to your life? _____

_____

_____

How do you have fun and play in your daily life? _____

_____

What else could you do to have more fun? _____

_____

Using your imagination, what could you have in your life if you took the time to create it? _____

_____

_____

_____

_____

The Dark Planet Pluto

You are walking on a dark planet. It is a small planet and far from the warmth of the sun. It is cold here and the ground is covered with black rocks and big, thick, bushy black trees. The sky is a sullen yellow-gray with black clouds. There are black birds flying between the trees. You sit down on a large branch in one of the thickly leaved trees. You can see volcanoes in the distance. The volcanoes are spouting red lava. They look like death and rebirth at the same time. You feel liberated as you watch the energy rushing up from the core of this little planet to spew forth like red blood, creating veins of lava rivers and capillaries of lava streams.

You climb on the back of a raven and he flies you through the Plutonian night sky. The wind is rushing under the raven's wings and across your face as you try to see where the raven is taking you. The raven flies faster as you soar through the trees and the black landscape of Pluto over the tall, thin and very black mountains. You are lost to linear time and space now and exist only in this place of raven's magic. You feel yourself being transformed as you fly on through the dark night sky, lit only by Pluto's moons. You are flying into the heart of the darkness now and everything becomes very black, like thick, dark velvet in front of your eyes. You trust your raven to take you through the darkness and back to the light.

As you fly deep into the heart of the darkness you hear a sound. Listen closely to this sound and note carefully what it represents to you. The air smells like patchouli and clove, orange, frankincense and black pepper. The raven lands and lets you off. You thank him for his safe passage. You look around and see a great stone building made of black stone. You approach the building and the black stone door. The door is very large and very heavy but you manage to pull it open enough to slip your body inside.

Once inside, you see what appears to be a theater. The theater is filled with black velvet chairs and black velvet curtains that cover the stage. You find yourself a comfortable chair near the center of the

The Dark Planet Pluto

theater and you sit down. The lights go down and you can only see shadows by the sparkly lights of the aisle runners. The lights look like small stars lined up in a row alongside the edge of the black velvet carpet that runs down the center aisle of the dark theater. You get comfortable in your chair just as the curtains begin to open. The heavy black velvet curtains split and begin to peel back, revealing a dark movie screen. The screen lights up as a scene begins to play itself out in front of you.

As the scene continues, you recognize yourself in the scene. You recognize the scene as something from your past. This scene is something from your past that is unresolved and needs to be released for you to truly be happy. Take a good look at this scene as it plays out on the movie screen of your dark theater. Notice where the scene takes place and who else is in the scene with you. Let the you of right now look at this scene and see what is really taking place there. Notice how the you of that movie scene is responding to the situation.

Stop the film at any place that you like and rewrite the script to include how the you of the movie scene could have responded instead, that might have gotten you better results for your own peace of mind. What positive thing could, the you in the movie, have done to make this scene a better situation? What limiting decision may have been made, that if it were disconnected, would allow all negative emotions around this scene to be released forever?

Replay the movie to include this new and more positive scene. Allow the players in the movie to act out and allow the you in the movie to respond with love. Replay the scene as many times as you need to, making the proper edits to make your movie better. When you have the scene the way you want it, go ahead and close the curtain on the stage and leave the theater.

You are once again, standing outside in the dark landscape of Pluto. The raven asks you to take a ride to another location. You climb on his

The Dark Planet Pluto

back and he flies you faster through the dark sky and then he wheels to the right. You can see a large meadow. As you approach the meadow, you notice its garden-like appearance. It holds small ponds in its lush, grassy, blanketed landscape. Life seems to be teeming in this area of the planet. New growth is everywhere as tiny flowers in multi-colors cover the grassy areas around the ponds. The flowers are unique and beautiful, like nothing you have ever seen before. They have petals in configurations of twelve and are unique in shape and design. The colors of the flowers are brilliant shades of turquoise and yellow-greens. They are fuchsia-purples and different blends of colors than you are normally used to seeing in flora. This part of the planet Pluto is truly awe-inspiring and magically beautiful!

The raven drops you in a grassy patch and then lands in a small golden bush. The raven then changes into a phoenix with feathers of many sparkling colors. The phoenix speaks to you of your secret mission. He reminds you to die to old stuff and be reborn. The phoenix reveals your fears. He educates and empowers you to heal so that your divine purpose will be revealed. He unveils your potential and teaches you to claim your power. You are quite suddenly free from linear consciousness and subjective time and space. You feel your fears being forced to the surface and transformed. You feel your body relax and become very, very calm. You walk over and look deeply into one of the little ponds. Its inky black waters reflect the stars. As you stare deep into the water, you can see your true self. You can see the you that you are becoming. You tell the you in the future that you will be walking into your own magnificence as you go forward with each day and each act of love and kindness. You can see the promise that your future holds for you in the shining you that is reflected in the waters of the Plutonian pond.

You can feel your own power rising up your spine like a wonderful fire that revitalizes and renews your body, mind and spirit. You thank the phoenix and his counterpart, the raven, for all of their good teachings as you leave the little dark planet, renewed, refreshed, revitalized, and re-empowered. Only as quick as you can, you may return to the room and your body. And only as soon as you are ready, you can go ahead and open your eyes.

Your Impression of Pluto

_____
_____
_____
_____
_____
_____
_____
_____
_____
_____
_____
_____
_____
_____
_____
_____
_____
_____
_____
_____
_____
_____
_____
_____
_____
_____
_____
_____
_____
_____
_____
_____
_____

The Dark Planet Pluto
Healing Questions

"You climb on the back of a raven and he flies you through the Plutonian night sky"

What scene from your life was played out for you in the dark theater?

_____

_____

_____

_____

_____

_____

_____

_____

_____

What unresolved issue appeared, and who else was involved in the scene? _____

_____

_____

_____

_____

_____

In what different way could the scene have been played out by you that would have gotten you better results or have made the situation easier to deal with? _____

_____

_____

_____

_____

_____

_____

The Dark Planet Pluto
Healing Questions

Was there a limiting decision made by you at the time of this event? If so, what was the decision made, that if it were disconnected, would allow all negative emotions around this scene to be released forever?

_____
_____
_____
_____
_____
_____
_____
_____
_____
_____

What lesson might you have been learning even if it were in a harsh manner and how are you stronger for having survived this event?

_____
_____
_____
_____
_____
_____
_____
_____
_____
_____
_____
_____

Star Children

You are lying on your back in a Native American healing lodge on a bearskin with your head in the west of the lodge. There is a shaman in the lodge with you. He is rattling, drumming and chanting. There is a depression in the center of the lodge and your feet are in this depression. It is known to the Native Americans as a sipapu. It is a gateway to the world of your ancestors. You feel yourself fall through your feet and down into the sipapu. It is as though you are sliding down a tunnel and into the Earth. You meet a raven who flies up beside you and asks you if you would like a ride and a guide to the lower worlds. You tell him that you would appreciate both and he flies underneath you. You find yourself riding on the back of the raven into the lower realms of Mother Earth. You can feel the protection of her nurturing belly as you travel through the Earth Mother. Raven tells you to be brave, that only good things will come of this. So you trust your raven to guide you safely through the realms of your ancestors.

As you continue your journey through the lower worlds on the raven's back, you notice that the tunnel has opened up into a vast landscape inside the belly of the Earth. You can see a far horizon and an inner light source. The raven flies you over mountains and valleys and into a very green canyon. He touches down in a beautiful garden and lets you off. The garden is lush and fills you with a feeling of peace and contentment. You thank your raven for guiding you to such a marvelous place. He tells you to listen to your heart while you are here and you will know the truth. He flies away and leaves you in your magical garden. You see a richly scrolled, white wrought iron bench. You walk over to the bench and sit down. You take off your shoes and run your feet through the cool green grass. You sit back and take a deep breath and let the tranquility of the garden fill you.

You see two beings of light approaching you from a distance. As they draw nearer, they appear to be angelic beings that are glowing as though lit from within. They seem to be full of little twinkle lights. They greet you and seem to be happy to see you. They ask you how

Star Children

you like living on planet Earth and if you are happy. They tell you that they are proud of you and that they think you are making good progress in your Earth walk. They tell you that your mission on Earth is a bigger one than you may be aware of. They ask you if you are ready to step up to a higher level now. If you are ready to step up and you would like to be part of their world, you can go ahead and get up off of the bench and approach them. If you are not ready or don't feel like this is part of your mission, you may stay on the bench.

Should you decide to step up, you will find that it is because you feel at home with these light beings and want to know more of their world. If you have stepped up, you may find that these beings and their world feel like home to you. If this is so, it may be because they are your true family. They embrace you and kiss your forehead. They wrap a net of stars around your head and it falls over your hair and down your back. They tell you to have strength because your mission is an important one.

They tell you that they have the power to clear you of all of the things that you no longer need in your life. You can feel your body chemistry changing as they initiate a restoration and resolution. You are at once connected to your true home world and your place of origin. You are aware of what have been your weak spots in your Earth walk. And what you need to do to heal them become very apparent. You can feel the vibrational healing from the light beings take effect. You can feel your being evolve and change, filling with enlightenment. Your chakras spin with light energy. You look down at your body and it is filled with light. You look like the angelic light beings and realize that you are one of them. That is, unless you have chosen to sit this one out and are still on the bench. If that is the case, know that you may be of a denser form and may take a bit longer to transform to a light being. Know that you will make those changes only as soon as you are ready to embrace the light within. Allow yourself to transform as slowly as you need. If you are a light being, you may be able to change at an accelerated rate, perhaps even at light speed. Let yourself make those changes now.

Star Children

Allow the angelic light beings to work their transformational magic on you. Feel the connection to your true home and the evolution of your being. Know that as soon as you are ready you may begin to complete the shift to a light body. Let the densities of your Earth lessons fall away as your being becomes filled with light and you are transformed to a light being.

The angelic beings have helped you to see yourself for who you truly are. You now begin to understand your true mission with the people of the Earth and are able and willing to help them shift to become beings of light and love. It is a big mission and calls for you to become as loving as you possibly can in your thoughts and words to yourself and others. To be filled with light is to be filled with love. You are now a being of pure love. Bask in this feeling, and let it flow through your being into every cell in your body and throughout your energetic field.

The raven has returned to take you back to the surface world of your planet. You thank the angelic beings for their healing and teachings. They hug you and kiss your cheek. They tell you that they look forward to seeing you again soon. They wish you well on your continuing mission. You climb on the raven's back and he flies you back across the vast landscape of the hills and valleys of the underworld. He flies you back up the tunnel to the surface and back into the lodge with the shaman.

The shaman is still drumming and praying over you as you return to your body and to the room. Only as soon as you can, go ahead and open your eyes.

Your Impression of Star

Star Children
Healing Questions

"You see two beings of the light approaching you from a distance. As they draw nearer, they appear to be angelic beings that are glowing as though lit from within"

Are you happy here on Earth? _____
_____

Did the angelic beings feel somehow familiar to you? Or were they totally alien? _____
_____
_____

Did you step up or stay seated on the bench? _____
_____

What are your weaknesses on your Earth walk? _____
_____
_____
_____
_____

What do you need to do to heal those weaknesses and evolve?___
_____
_____
_____
_____

What is your true mission on the Earth? _____
_____
_____
_____
_____
_____

Star Children
Healing Questions

In what ways have the trials in your life prepared you to be better able to handle the situations that may be involved in your true mission? _____

_____

_____

_____

_____

_____

_____

What are you doing currently for the people of planet Earth?

_____

_____

_____

What more can you do to be of service to your planet and your people?_____

_____

_____

_____

How can love make the Earth a better home? _____

_____

_____

_____

_____

_____

_____

_____

_____

The Goddess Sedna

You can feel an icy wind whipping across your face, and you can hear the booming of the large commercial fishing vessel as it cuts a path through icy seas. You are in the vast wilderness of the Arctic Seas. There are tall glacial mountains rising up out of the ocean. On the surface of the water, there are large chunks of ice floating about that dot the liquid landscape. You hear the captain of the ship yell something in a loud voice. Men are scurrying across the deck. You look over the rail and see a pod of several large Orca, or killer whales that are swimming alongside the ship. They are rolling their huge bodies over and under the surface of the water. They seem to be playing a game of tag with each other as they slice through the water. You feel honored to be gifted with their joyous presence. You overhear one of the men onboard mention that he hopes that Sedna will bless them with a good haul this season.

The ship drops anchor outside of a small fishing village and some of the men are going ashore in a large dory. You decide to join them and jump into the dory and find a seat. Once on shore, you notice that the people here seem to be Native American. You walk into a small old building that appears to be a bait and tackle, general store and cafe all rolled into one quaint location. The Native lady behind the counter tells you that she is an Inuit and offers to tell you the Myth of Sedna.

You pull up a chair and listen closely as she describes the beautiful Inuit girl, named Sedna, who was too vain to marry just anyone. She spends her days combing her hair and putting off suitors. Finally, her father promises her hand to a hunter, and she has to marry him. The Inuit lady tells you how Sedna left her village with her new husband only to discover that he was really a raven. The raven takes Sedna to a far island where she is isolated and lonely. She cries for her father to rescue her from this awful fate, and finally her father does so. He comes to the island in a kayak, and Sedna gets into the boat. They begin to row across the water toward home when the raven spies them and chases after them. The raven begins to attack Sedna's father, who becomes so afraid that he pushes Sedna

The Goddess Sedna

overboard. She tries to hang on to the side of the kayak but her father hits her hands with the paddle. She sinks to the bottom, leaving her fingers on the side of the boat. Sedna's fingers, while sinking to the bottom, turn into seals and whales. Sedna becomes the goddess of the sea and all of its creatures. The whales and seals become her companions. The Inuit lady tells you that, to this day, respect must be given to Sedna in the ways of the hunters if they want a successful hunt. If they anger her, she will withhold the sea creatures and bring storms until the hunters become respectful of her once again. The Inuit Shamans dive deep into the icy waters and comb the sea kelp that is Sedna's hair. Appeasing her so that she will bring good weather and a bountiful hunt. You thank the Inuit lady for her story and tell her that respecting this beautiful place, Sedna's world and her sea creatures is a wonderful message to our planet.

You leave the little store and find a snowy path behind it that leads into the forest. You decide to follow the path and see where it might lead you. You are glad for the warm anorak jacket with the fur trim and down lining that you chose to wear as it permits you to feel perfectly comfortable on your hike through this frozen wilderness. As you are walking, you can feel the crunch of the icy snow under your boots. You take a step, and the path seems to give way underneath you. You slip down into a hole. You are slipping through a dark, watery tunnel and yet you feel perfectly calm as your body slides through this dark, smooth tunnel. You seem to be moving at an incredible pace almost as if you were shooting through a black hole in outer space.

Suddenly, you fall into a snowy landscape, much like the area that you were hiking through, but it feels different somehow. You see a shoreline and you walk toward it. Out of the sea come several seals and dolphins. They seem to shape shift into a group of grandmothers. They sit down at a table that seems to be made of whalebone and shell. One of them puts a starfish on the table. They begin to laugh and tell stories from the old days of the old ways. You approach the table and take a seat beside one of the grandmothers. She puts the

The Goddess Sedna

starfish into your hand and tells you not to be afraid of the shifts that are coming for planet Earth. She tells you that this planet, the planet Sedna, is influencing the collapse on Earth in order to bring about the needed evolutionary changes for the planet Earth and its people. The grandmothers begin to speak of a mourning of the old ways that are really the modern ways of today. They speak of a return to the new ways that are really the very ancient ways. They speak to you of the respect that is needed at this time for all of the mothers and grandmothers. They tell you that it is the love and nurturing of these mothers and grandmothers that is currently holding the chaos in check on planet Earth. They tell you to stand solidly in this time of melt and thaw. They tell you to shift your inner spinal pole as the pole of the Earth shifts so that you can adapt to the Earth changes. You thank them for their messages as you watch them return to their sea-creature forms and slide back into the icy ocean.

You continue walking away from the shoreline and toward a large glacial mountain. You see an ice cave in the side of the mountain and decide to investigate. Inside of the ice cave is a large rock statue of huge boulders piled one on top of the other, forming a rock cairn in the shape of a human being. The rock seems to come to life and transforms itself into a beautiful woman with long flowing black hair. She tells you that she is the Goddess Sedna and that she has come to do work on you. She motions to a slab of ice, and you lie down on the ice table. She begins to work on you by fanning you with a large piece of whalebone. It is a whale's jaw that is painted with stars and planets. The teeth are Herkimer diamonds. She is putting more of these Herkimer diamonds on your body. They seem to fall through you into the places in your body that need healing. She turns you over and begins to place more of these stones on your spine. They fall into your spinal column and begin a subtle shift in the cellular format of your spine. She places one on your crown chakra that fills your head with light. You can feel the subtle shifting in your spinal column and a subtle change in the motion and rhythm of your spinal fluid as Sedna's magic takes effect. Your body is shining like the sun on the surface of the cold arctic waters of Earth. Sedna tells you to forgive those people whose pollution will bring about the global

The Goddess Sedna

warming and the glacial collapse. She says that without their lessons we would not have brought about this new shift. She asks you to be compassionate and forgiving to those who will be unable to ride the new wave. She tells you that with this shift comes a new frequency which will allow the people to evolve their consciousness to collectively create a new reality for the people of planet Earth. You begin to dream the dream of Sedna, and you hear an inner sound ...listen...the inner sound is the maker of light. The inner sound comes from the Creator and teaches you to create with respect and responsibility. You begin to lay down a new architecture.

Outside of the ice cave, you see a group of Native fishermen who are holding the edges of a large net with long-handled arrows. Sedna tells you that they are the Sketiu and that they are weaving the net of the universe. You come out of the ice cave and join the Sketiu. They hand you an arrow and ask you to hold a piece of the net. You notice that, as you hold the net with the arrow, you are able to move energy through the net just by thinking about where you want the energy to go. You find that you are able to weave the net, yet not become ensnared in it, as long as you use the arrow. The Sketiu tell you that they are weaving a new reality for planet Earth. They invite you to weave your own new reality. You realize that the net is a hologram of not only the Earth but also of your body, and you can reweave any sections that are torn or knotted and make them like new. So you take a few moments to do this, reweaving in all of the places in your body and soul that need it.

The Sketiu seem to be weaving the intergalactic fabric of space as you watch their deft fingers work. You can see the planets and other celestial bodies contained with the star lines of this galactic net. The planets are connected through this net of star lines and seem to be communicating with each other through these star lines. The planets suddenly turn into great gemstones that are conducting energy along the star lines of the net. The gemstones appear to be lighting up as the energy from these star lines reaches them. The Sketiu tell you that you are beginning to understand now, and one of them puts a fire agate in your hand. They walk toward the shoreline and turn into a group of sea lions. They jump into the ocean and swim away.

The Goddess Sedna

You walk back into the ice cave and seem to slip down into a black hole again. You slide through the dark tunnel back to the spot on the path that you were hiking, that lies behind the general store. You walk back to the beach and look for the ship that you came in on. You see a giant wave that seems to be riding on the back of another giant wave. It is rising up out of a stormy sea. All sea life has gone deep now to wait out the storm. A great sound is heard, and the frequency of this sound travels through the waters of planet Earth, reawakening the ancient spirit of Mother Earth. Her name is Gaia. She begins to sing along with this great sound. The sound is heard and the resulting sound wave is felt, first by all of the creatures of the sea and then by the sea birds. The sound is heard and felt by the polar bears and then the black and brown bears, musk ox to bison, eagle, coyote and even mouse. All the creatures of the Earth, even the human beings, are affected by this soliton sound wave. All humans who are ready and willing will feel the shift now within the spinal pole of their bodies as they begin to shift along with the poles of planet Earth.

The sea lion, seals, whales and dolphins come out to play as the wave recedes and the re-emergence of life after the emergency begins anew. The storm-cleansed waters are smooth and calm now. You feel reborn on every level. Everything has rebalanced in this wave. You see the ship that you came in on returning to the shore. A dory comes your way, and the men wave you into the boat and take you back to their ship. Once again, you are standing on the deck of this huge vessel as it makes its way across the Arctic Sea.

Bringing back with you all of the gifts and messages of Sedna, you may now return to the room and to your body and only as soon as you can, you may open your eyes.

Your Impression of Sedna

The Goddess Sedna
Healing Questions

"Out of the sea come several seals and dolphins. They seem to shape shift into a group of grandmothers. They sit down at a table that seems to be made of whale bone and shell. One of them puts a starfish on the table. They begin to laugh and tell stories from the old days and the old ways."

In what ways are you respectful to the women around you? Are there ways that you could be respectful of the women in your life? _____
_____
_____
_____

If you are a woman, are you respectful of your own feelings? _____
_____
_____

How do you treat yourself?_____

Do you ask for the same respect from others?_____
_____

Will others respect you more if you respect yourself more?_____
_____

In what ways could you be more respectful to yourself and thereby teach others how to treat you with respect?_____
_____
_____
_____
_____
_____
_____

The Goddess Sedna
Healing Questions

Why are our mothers and grandmothers so important? What do you think is the lesson that they have for us? _____

_____

_____

_____

What could you do to respect the Earth Mother and protect her?

_____

_____

Do you recycle? What other ways can you help save the planet in your own way? _____

_____

_____

_____

If there was one thing that you could thank your own Mother and/or Grandmother for, what would that be? _____

_____

_____

_____

What do you think is the hardest part about being a good Mother?

_____

_____

_____

How could you be more responsible for the sea and the sea creatures of planet Earth? _____

_____

_____

_____

The Goddess Sedna
Healing Questions

Make a list of all the things you use in your life that add to the pollution of this planet. Which ones can you eliminate from your life? Synthetic fabrics, stain resistant fabric, waterproofing, flame retardants, etc., etc._____

_____

_____

_____

_____

_____

_____

What things were healed for you by the Goddess Sedna? _____

_____

_____

_____

_____

What things were healed by reweaving the nets of your body with the Sketiu? _____

_____

_____

_____

_____

Could you feel the spinal realignment take place? _____

_____

_____

_____

The Sun God

You are flying through the cosmos, following a star line, in your personal spacecraft. The solar winds are blowing as your spacecraft approaches the great gaseous body of the sun. Your ship is pulled into the vastness of the sun and you appear to be moving safely within some kind of bubble. You arrive at a large golden temple, the temple of the sun. Your ship lands on a landing pad that seems to be a large slab of golden marble. You set down gently and step out of your ship. You see the large palace doors of the sun temple open, beckoning you in. You walk inside of the sun temple and are greeted by the Sun God. He says his name is Ra. He is an imposing figure with golden skin stretched tight over a strong and athletic body. He wears a golden tunic and golden sandals. He has a circlet of gold on his head with three stones set in it, sunstones that rest on his brow.

Ra invites you to come in and join him. This temple is made of golden marble with golden marble pillars and floors. There are large carnelian sun discs set on either side of Ra's great throne. His golden throne is actually a chariot. This chariot is pulled across the sky by winged golden stallions. You see, as he sits on his throne, the look of responsibility that crosses Ra's face. He seems to take his job very seriously with little or no room for error. He has a sense of great urgency to take action and get things done. You are at once immersed in a feeling of power and capability. You can feel the vital energy of this place running up your spine as though your spinal fluid has become infused with a power drink that fills you with confidence. Your body is warm and feels alive with the revitalizing power of the Sun God Ra emanating around and through you.

Ra seems to be a great leader, who is capable of both strength and honesty. He gifts you with those things as he sits before you on his throne. So take those gifts into yourself and let strength, originality and honesty become yours now. Ra smiles at you, and you smile back. You feel as though you are unable to stop smiling. You feel your heart filling with joy and laughter. Ra looks at you quizzically and with great amusement, and you both break into simultaneous laughter. He claps

The Sun God

you on the back and tells you that you will do well with the powers that he has bestowed upon you. You at once understand your individuality and independence and how powerful they can be for you.

He hands you a small vial of oil. It is hung on a string and he tells you to put it around your neck. He says that the vial contains essence of the sun itself. He tells you to put it around your neck, and you do so. He says that this vial of sunlight will revitalize you whenever you need it, all you have to do is smell it. He invites you to do so now. You open your vial of oil and take a deep breath of the heady oil. It smells like lemon, lime and grapefruit, cedar wood, neroli, helichrysum, frankincense and myrrh. It is immediately refreshing and renewing. Your body surges with the strength of the sun. Your heart, back and spine are healed of old discomforts. You can feel the regenerative powers of Ra and the sun moving through your body, inside and out.

Ra throws your spacecraft into the back of his throne/chariot and tells you to hop in. He says that he will give you a lift home. You step into his golden chariot and the winged golden stallions transport you across the sky and back to Earth. You thank Ra for his most amazing gifts of strength, originality, honesty, vivaciousness, expertise and courage. You thank him for showing you your true power. You step out of the chariot and back onto Earth, into the room and into your body. You may open you eyes as soon as you are ready with all of your gifts intact.

Your Impression of The Sun

_____

_____

_____

_____

_____

_____

_____

_____

_____

_____

_____

_____

_____

_____

_____

_____

_____

_____

_____

_____

_____

_____

_____

_____

_____

_____

_____

The Sun God
Healing Questions

"You arrive at a large golden temple, the temple of the Sun"

In what ways in your life could you be more honest? _____
_____
_____
_____
_____

Why is it important to lead others with strength, originality and
honesty? _____
_____
_____
_____

How could you put these traits to work for you in your relationships
and interactions with others? _____
_____
_____
_____

In what ways did the revitalizing energies of the Sun heal you?
_____
_____
_____

In what ways could you be more independent and responsible for
yourself in your life? _____
_____
_____
_____
_____

The Sun God
Healing Questions

What could you do right now to start taking more responsibility for your situation in life and be more independent? _____

_____

_____

_____

_____

_____

_____

_____

How does being generous serve you? _____

_____

_____

_____

_____

_____

In what ways do you consider yourself an expert, and how does thi make you more confident? _____

_____

_____

_____

_____

_____

_____

_____

_____

_____

Planetary Aspects of Healing

Mercury - Helps you with communication issues with yourself and others. It helps you to communicate with your inner self and inner guides. It calms your nervous system and brings focus. It makes you more alert to the situations at hand. It revitalizes you in the face of trials and allows you to give yourself more choices about how you do things in your life.

Venus - Helps you to be more loving in all areas of your life. Helps you to learn to cooperate and create collectively. Allows you to become healthier and happier through responding with love in all things. Helps you to learn to appreciate all of the special gifts in yourself and in your life. Helps you to know when you are truly loved and appreciated.

Earth/Ohm - Helps ground you into your body and connect you to the earth. Helps you to support yourself and create a supporting environment for yourself and those around you. Helps you to find clarity and be open spiritually to loving yourself and fulfilling your own needs so that you can be there for those who need you.

The Moon - Brings feminine nurturing to those who need it. Helps to regulate all of the cycles in your life. Helps to balance body waters and helps to release edemas and inflammations as well as regulate blood flow and spinal fluid flow and rhythm. Helps to increase your psychic vision. Helps you to let go of old cycles and patterns that no longer serve or protect you.

Mars - Helps to release grief and loss issues. Helps release traumas and purge unnecessary baggage. Helps you to regain courage and fortitude through the trials in your life. Helps you to find new solutions and directions with determination. Helps you to take responsibility for all of your creations and recreate what you don't like about your life to something that makes you happy.

Planetary Aspects of Healing, continued

Jupiter - Helps you to be more understanding and tolerant of others and their actions. We are all in this world struggling together to find some joy and peace. Helps you to be more optimistic and productive. Helps you to expand your consciousness and ways of self-expression. Helps you to be more efficient and successful. Helps you to solve problems without anger, using logic instead.

Saturn - Helps you find maturity through self-knowledge and self-awareness. Helps you to set healthy boundaries with self-trust and self-control. Helps you to find solidity within yourself and be able to trust others.

Chiron - Helps with release of back and neck pain and tension. Helps to realign the spine and hips. Helps to open disc space. Helps release fear of success and self-sabotaging behaviors. Helps you to be more free to make commitments. Helps to keep you stable on your journey.

Uranus - Helps with originality and creativity. Helps to initiate big changes in your life. Opens you to the unexpected and the unknown. Helps to revitalize all of the electrical and neurological systems in your body. Opens and sends light to all of the chakras in the body. Help you to make changes with conscious intent in regard to your life. Helps you to be the conductor of your own symphony/galaxy. Helps release lower body pain.

Neptune - Helps bring the body and mind to complete relaxation. Helps to release mysterious illnesses and pain. Helps you to become the mystic and the psychic visionary. Helps to rebalance all of the body's systems on all levels. Helps to rebalance the rhythmic flow of the spinal fluid. Helps to release old deceptions and illusions, and helps you to be more imaginative. Helps to remind you to play.

Pluto - Helps to release and resolve fear issues that have plagued you throughout your life. Allows you let go and rewrite those old traumas and allow yourself forward movement. Opens you to

Planetary Aspects of Healing, continued

releasing limiting decisions that may have been made in the past that no longer serve or protect you. Helps you to get the lesson behind unresolved issues. (Why would I chose to teach myself in this way, and what did I learn as a result of this lesson choice?) Whether you think that you are a victim or not, you chose to learn in this way. There are no victims, only lessons.

Star - Helps to re-encode the DNA to a higher evolution. Returns your heart to home. Helps you to become a light being. Resolves and restores your body to a light body. Helps you to discover your true mission on the Earth. Helps you to look at your weaknesses and find new strength and new ways of doing things.

Sedna - Helps you to respect yourself and others. Helps you learn to respect women and all of the gifts that they bring. Teaches you to honor the Grandmothers and all of their love and teachings. Helps you to learn to protect the Earth and the oceans and all of the creatures of the Earth and sea. Helps you to be more ecologically minded. Helps bridge the gap between nature and technology and living in both worlds at the same time. Helps with amputations. Helps with severing of family ties. Helps with fear of global collapse and global warming. Helps to realign you to accept a new polar position for the Earth and new spinal pole position for you to revolve and evolve around.

Sun - Helps you to find confidence and generosity as a way to respond to your daily trials. Helps you to become more independent and honest in your interactions with yourself and others. Helps you to revitalize and be more vivacious and powerful. Helps you to own being the expert at things that you really excel at. Helps you to create your life with responsibility for all that you create to learn from in your life. Helps release pain and promotes healing of the heart, back and spine. Regenerates and warms all systems in the body.

About The Author

Michelle Marie Many is a holistic health practitioner, hypnotherapist, emotional counselor, sound healer and body worker. Currently she resides in the Vail Valley area of Colorado. She facilitates women's retreats all over the United States and teaches conferences and workshops.

Michelle is a Chippewa Indian from the Turtle Mountain Clan of North Dakota. She is an apprentice and student in the Native American healing arts with such wonderful teachers as David Carson, author of his million selling, "The Medicine Cards" and "Crossing Into Medicine Country", and his latest work "Oracle 2013". David has taken Michelle under his wing and brought her into his Choctaw Clan of the Carson family. He has taken her to Sundances and Sacred Sites. Michelle is learning Animal Medicine from him. Michelle and David have taught workshops and conferences together in Colorado and New Mexico.

Michelle is currently apprenticing with a Cherokee Grandmother and supreme crystal worker, Grandmother Jean Bustos. Together they have taught women's retreats and women's empowerment circles, and have done crystal healings together.

Noted astrologer and author of such books as "Glimpses" and "The Sun at the Center", Philip Sedgwick has been helping Michelle broaden her knowledge of astrology. Michelle has been Philip's student and friend for several years.

Donna Carey is the founder of Kairos Sound Institute and has given the world the Acutonics Planetary Tuning Forks and Gongs. Michelle has trained at the advanced level and has been working with the Acutonics Tuning Forks since 2003. It was in Judy Bernard's level three Acutonics class during the planetary gong attunements, that "The Planetary Meditations" were conceived. As each planet's frequency was gonged into Michelle's body, she received powerful visions of lush imagery that became, "The Planetary Meditations".

About The Author, continued

Michelle does her own singing on several of the recordings of the meditations on CD. She plays flute, the mark tree chimes, rainsticks, tambourines and various other rattles and tinklers as well as the tuning forks and singing bowls. Joe Romersa plays ahbe's (eden ahbez) personal calf-skin barrol drums on several tracks. Joe plays all of the other instruments, including acoustic guitar, electric bass, keyboards, sitar, a bodran drum, a standard drum set and cymbals, rattles, and various other percussive instruments. Joe did the sound engineering and all of the beautiful graphics and formatting of the book.

Michelle currently resides in Colorado in a small town, high in the Rocky Mountains, where she continues her private practice as well as her women's retreats, conferences and workshops. She is married to David Many and they share their home with an extra large bear-like Newfoundland dog named Orion and Michelle's black cat of over 17 years, Ravenwind; as well as a vast array of wild critters and a national forest.

For more information or to order "The Planetary Meditations", or for new meditations on CD with book sets, contact Holistic Mountain and Michelle Many:

Holistic Mountain
www.holisticmountain.com
970-949-7458
PO Box 64
Red Cliff, CO 81649

Acknowledgements

I wish to acknowledge and thank my mother Carol Diane Lorentzen and my Grandmother Marie Louise Decouteau Lorentzen for my bloodlines, teachings and inspirations from Native America. I would like to thank Jack Quinn, the only father that I have ever really known. I would like to thank my aunt Betty and my uncle Larry for helping to parent me. I thank my cousins, Jerry Reese and Cindy (Reese) Opsteegh with whom I was raised. I would also like to thank my husband Dave Many for sticking with me throughout the creative process; your a good man honey.

I would very much like to thank my marvelous partner in this project, Joe Romersa, a brilliant musician, sound engineer, composer and artist, without whom this series would not be what it is. I would like to thank eden ahbez, or ahbe to his friends, --The original "Nature Boy"--for his guidance and inspiration from the ethers.

I am very appreciative to Kairos Sound Institute and Donna Carey for the Acutonics Planetary Tuning Forks, Gongs, and Wind Chimes what a priceless treasure these tools are for healing. I thank my teachers and mentors for all of their wonderful knowledge and patience. These teachers are Donna Carey, Ellen Franklin, Catherine Birch Story and Judy Bernard from the Kairos Sound Institute. I would like to thank and acknowledge David Carson, Grandmother Jean Bustos and Philip Sedgwick. You are all gifts and angels in my life.